Make It HAPPEN!

Stephen Ritz

URBAN FARMER

Green Bronx Machine Blvd

BY HEATHER WILLIAMS

Lightswitch
LEARNING

150 East 52nd Street, Suite 32002
New York, NY 10022
www.lightswitchlearning.com

Educators and Librarians, for a variety of teaching resources, visit www.lightswitchlearning.com

Library of Congress Cataloging-in-Publication Data is available upon request.
Library of Congress Catalog Card Number pending

SBN: 978-1-68265-615-0

Stephen Ritz by Heather Williams

Edited by Lauren Dupuis-Perez
Book design by Sara Radka
The text of this book is set in Neuton Regular.

Printed in Republic of Korea

Image Credits

Cover: Green Bronx Machine
Page 1: Same as cover
Page 4: Green Bronx Machine
Page 5: Green Bronx Machine
Page 5: Green Bronx Machine
Page 5: Green Bronx Machine
Page 6: Green Bronx Machine

Page 7: Green Bronx Machine
Page 8: Green Bronx Machine
Page 10: Pixabay
Page 11: Shutterstock
Page 12: Green Bronx Machine
Page 14: Green Bronx Machine
Page 15: Green Bronx Machine

Page 16: Green Bronx Machine
Page 18: Green Bronx Machine
Page 19: Green Bronx Machine
Page 20: Green Bronx Machine
Page 22: Green Bronx Machine
Page 23: Green Bronx Machine
Page 24: Green Bronx Machine
Page 26: Shutterstock

"My students inspire me way more than I inspire them. They give me energy!"

Stephen Ritz

. . .

Make It! HAPPEN!

Before Reading

Think about your own goals. Do you want to play soccer or make music? All of these activities take time and practice.

During Reading

During reading, review the highlighted vocab words. While learning about Stephen, understand how he got to where he is today. What **skills** has he shown that have helped his **career**? In each chapter, the Make It Happen! activity will help you, too, build skills to reach your own goals.

After Reading

Look in the back of the book for questions and activities to help you think about Stephen's story. Share these with a friend, parent, or teacher. Also, talk about the skills you need to reach your goals.

skill: the ability to do something that comes from training, experience, or practice

career: a job or profession that someone does for a long time

Contents

Early Life

Even as a child, Stephen liked to wear a bow tie.

Stephen Ritz grew up and worked within the unique world of the Bronx.

It was a hot August morning in the Bronx, New York, in 1984. A tall, thin man walked quickly down St. Ann's Avenue. His name was Stephen Ritz. He was hurrying to his first teaching job at South Bronx High School. He was only 21 years old.

At first, Stephen's students didn't trust him. On his first day, he asked a student named Vanessa to sit down. "What do you know about what we go through?" she asked. "You're here to get paid. Go home!" But Stephen didn't go home. Instead, he shared his lunch with Vanessa. The two became lifelong friends. This was the first step on a journey that would transform Stephen into a teacher like no other.

The Bronx Is Home

Stephen Ritz was born and raised in the Bronx. When he was young, Stephen learned to interact with **diverse** people and points of view. "There is no place on Earth like the Bronx," said Stephen. "My friends' families were Irish, Italian, Jewish, and African," he said. In the Bronx, Stephen learned the importance of **teamwork**. Whenever Stephen or his friends needed help or advice, there was always someone who could lend them a hand.

The Bronx was also where Stephen went to elementary school. Stephen didn't get very good grades. "For me, school wasn't just about my classes," Stephen said. Stephen loved to learn, but didn't always like the way he was being taught. He also loved to play basketball. School, parks, and **community centers** were Stephen's favorite places.

diverse: made up of many different types of people

teamwork: the working together of a group of people in order to achieve something

community center: a place where people can gather for activities

Stephen didn't enjoy **academics**. This later helped him become an **innovator**. He became the kind of teacher who could change students' lives.

academics: the classes taken at school or in college

innovator: someone who uses a new idea or method of doing something

Make It HAPPEN! Ask for Help

Asking for help takes courage. Growing up in the Bronx, Stephen and his friends relied on their community for support, ideas, and supplies.

Make a list of things you want to do that you need help with. Then make a list of people who could help you. Be ready to listen to people's advice, and don't give up!

Not sure where to start? Here are some ideas:

- Ask a coach to help you improve your athletic skills.
- Ask your teacher for help in a subject that isn't your best.
- Ask a trusted friend or adult to support your interests.
- Ask a teacher or other adult to help you start a club.

What was the hardest part about asking for advice? How did it help you reach your goal?

First Steps
of the Journey

Stephen knew that his students would connect with nature if he brought it into the classroom. He started with fish.

After college, Stephen wanted to play professional basketball. When he hurt his knee, he had to stop playing. Instead, he became a teacher in the Bronx. He loved the job. He shared hip-hop, snacks, and personal stories with students. This helped him to "connect with students and kept them coming to class," he said. Students like Vanessa began to respect him.

Daffodils start growing in the spring when the ground begins to warm up.

Stephen asked his friends for help with his science class. One morning, he received a box. It was filled with what looked like moldy onions. Disappointed, he hid them behind a radiator in his classroom. Six weeks later, daffodils were growing in the box!

The flowers **inspired** Stephen and his students. They planted thousands of flowers around New York City. They also started a group called Green Teens.

inspire: to give another person the idea or confidence to try something new

Part of the Solution

The Green Teens wanted to help their neighbors. They decided to grow food as well as flowers. At a gardening show in California, Stephen found an **invention** that changed his life. This new way of gardening would also fix his class's space issue. It was called the Tower Garden. A Tower Garden can grow 28 plants in a small space. This was the answer to his classroom gardening dreams!

Tower Gardens help small spaces have enough room for big gardens.

Stephen and his students grew herbs and vegetables in the Tower Gardens. His class realized the importance of fresh food. They also learned the benefits of teamwork.

invention: a new tool or device that someone came up with to serve a purpose

They were featured on several TV programs, and on Disney Channel's *Pass the Plate*. The Green Teens' success also led to the creation of two important projects. These are the Green Bronx Machine and the National Health, Wellness, and Learning Center.

Make It HAPPEN! Grow Your Own Plant

Stephen Ritz and his students grew many different kinds of plants. Use your **initiative** and try planting something yourself in your home!

You will need:

- Seeds: Do you want to grow a flower, fruit, or vegetable? You can buy seeds in a garden center, hardware store, or online. Get an adult to help you.

- A soda bottle, milk carton, empty can, or small flower pot.

- Potting soil. This can be purchased with your seeds at a garden center, hardware store, or online!

Research your plant on the internet. How much light and water does it need? Follow the instructions on the seed packet for planting.

Write down your plant's progress. How long did it take for your plant to start growing?

Overcoming
Obstacles

GROW SOMETHING

GREATER!!

Stephen finds many fun ways to inspire people with his words.

When Stephen is faced with a challenge, he sees it as an **opportunity**. He couldn't play basketball, so he started teaching. He sometimes disagreed with principals and other teachers, but he kept doing what he thought was right. Today, Stephen's motto is "*¡Sí se puede!*" or "Yes, we can!"

In 2017, students were able to eat salads that they grew themselves.

> **opportunity:** a chance to do something you wouldn't otherwise get to do
>
> **exceed:** to go beyond or be greater than something

Stephen and his students have all faced hard times. Stephen's wife Lizette became pregnant with twins. One died very early in the pregnancy. The other was born too early and passed away. Stephen and his family were heartbroken. However, "we wanted our son's legacy to **exceed** his short time on Earth," Stephen said. Stephen and his wife started a foundation that supports children all over the world. They support many charities.

Setbacks and New Opportunities

Poor health can also be an obstacle in life. For years, Stephen ate fast food and junk food, and drank sodas. As a result, he became overweight and had several health problems. Then, he almost had a heart attack. He passed out at school and woke up at the hospital. Stephen realized, "If I was going to teach my students to lead healthier lives, shouldn't I do the same?" Stephen lost over 100 pounds in 7 months! He taught his students how to form healthy habits.

Many of his students faced obstacles every day, from learning challenges to extreme **poverty** to violence at school and in the community. But Stephen learned, "When we teach children about nature, we teach them to **nurture**."

Stephen celebrated every pound he lost as he became healthier and healthier.

poverty: the state of being very poor

nurture: to take care of or help something or someone grow or succeed

One day, Stephen discovered that Vanessa had a drug problem. He promised to help her, and he kept his promise. It inspired her to help others.

Make It HAPPEN!

How Healthy Do You Eat?

Stephen ate a lot of unhealthy foods for a long time. Research the nutrition of your favorite foods. Think about ways to improve your diet.

You will need:

- A computer
- Internet access

1. Think of the foods you eat most often. Write down two or three of them.

2. Research how much of certain vitamins you need every day. For example, how much vitamin C does a person your age need daily?

3. See how much each food provides. The food might not have a Nutrition Information panel on the packaging. Use the internet to look it up.

How nutritious are the foods on your list? Ask a parent or other adult for help finding foods that give you the vitamins you need to stay healthy.

Teamwork

At a conference in 2017, Stephen met with Tim Blank, the developer of Tower Gardens.

Through his entire teaching career, Stephen's family has supported him. His mother encouraged him to take the test to get his teaching **license**. His wife Lizette has been his biggest supporter. She even helped drive students to events. She always helps Stephen with projects. Their daughter Michaela also joined in with some of Stephen's projects. She was like a little sister to Stephen's students.

Stephen's wife and daughter have been with him on this journey from the beginning.

Stephen loves his students. He considers them to be family. He stays in touch with many of them. "When I see students with their parents, grandparents, and family, I want them to feel the passion, purpose, and hope that I have for everybody," Stephen said.

license: an official document that gives a person permission to do something

Supporters

Stephen gives his students the credit for his success. They needed a special kind of teacher. This **motivated** Stephen to teach **creatively**. "My students inspire me way more than I inspire them," Stephen said. "They give me energy!"

Viraj Puri's company Gotham Greens grows vegetables on rooftops.

One student, Alberto, was good with computers. But he had learning challenges. Stephen helped Alberto become the school's first **technology specialist**. Stephen's student Vanessa helped him, as well. She showed him how to connect learning to his students' lives. Together, they learned the value of second chances.

Many people have helped Stephen achieve his goals. Stan Zucker was Stephen's professor.

motivate: to inspire someone to work hard and be successful

creatively: using imagination to think of new ideas

technology: machines or other tools that were developed using scientific knowledge in order to solve problems

specialist: someone who has skill or knowledge about a specific thing; an expert

He helped Stephen learn to never give up on students. Viraj Puri runs an **urban farming** company called Gotham Greens. He helped Stephen and his students create a **hydroponic** garden.

urban farming: growing food in a city or town

hydroponic: relating to a method of gardening where plants are grown in water rather than soil

Make It HAPPEN! Start a Club

Stephen and his students started Green Teens because they were excited about improving their neighborhood and planting flowers. Start your own club at school and get your classmates involved in an activity that interests you!

- Choose a theme. Pick something you love, such as a sport or hobby.
- Talk to a teacher or other adult. Does your school have any rules about clubs?
- Ask a friend for help. You can be the club's president. Your friend can be the vice president. Find three more friends to be the first club members!
- Ask a teacher, counselor, coach, or parent to be your **advisor**.

What was difficult about forming your club? How can you improve your club in the future?

advisor: a person who gives opinions and suggestions to someone about what to do

Current Career

Stephen has set up Tower Gardens all over the United States and in many parts of the world. Here, he is visiting True Gardens in Mesa, Arizona.

Stephen enjoys sharing his story. He speaks at schools and organizations around the world. He tells people about Green Bronx Machine and **sustainable** living. Stephen also wrote a book. It is called *The Power of a Plant*. It became a bestseller! In it, Stephen talks about his students and their journey. He explains how growing plants taught him to help people. First, Stephen planted flowers with his students. Soon, the class's projects became "an engine for community change." Green Bronx Machine was born. It supports green classroom projects all over the world, and provides **innovative** activities for students seven days a week.

Stephen even brought his planting knowledge to the White House.

sustainable: able to not use up the Earth's natural resources

innovative: using a new idea or method in order to do something

Learning and Growing

Teaching skills in the kitchen is an important part of health and wellness education.

For years, Stephen had a dream of opening his own school. He started the National Health, Wellness, and Learning Center in the Bronx. The Learning Center has seven Tower Gardens. It also has a kitchen. It has exercise bikes that **generate** electricity. It also has special technology for teaching. At the center, Stephen's students "make **epic** happen" every day. They cook and eat the food they grow. They give food to the community. His students are learning how to be healthy. They give back to their neighborhood.

Teaching and helping his students grow is Stephen's most important job. Now Vanessa, Stephen's former student, runs a program of her own. "Mr. Ritz taught me that people are like plants,

generate: to produce or create something, such as energy

epic: very important, wonderful, or exciting; going beyond what is normal or ordinary

they need love, water, and some bright light to grow and be successful," Vanessa said. "Every day, Stephen and his students are driven to work hard and make it happen for students in the Bronx and around the world!"

Make It HAPPEN! Write a Journal Entry

Stephen Ritz's book *The Power of a Plant* is filled with personal stories. It tells about Stephen's experiences in his community and his classroom. Be creative and write a journal entry about a story in your own life.

Some things to consider:

- Your story should be something that means a lot to you. It could be about a school year, a sports season, or even a single day.
- Focus the story on you and your experience, even if it involves other people.
- Since you are telling a true story, you will need to include some facts. What do you remember? What stood out to you?

Why did you choose to write about this particular event or moment? Share your story with friends or family.

Defining Moments

Stephen Ritz used his passion for learning and his love of his community to build gardens. These gardens gave his students healthy food and a purpose.

2011

Stephen founds the Green Bronx Machine with the help of his students.

2012

Stephen becomes a White House Champion of Change and loses 100 pounds!

2013

Stephen and the Green Bronx Machine appear on Disney's *Pass the Plate*. This show helps inspire kids to eat healthy.

2014

Stephen brings Tower Gardens to schools across America.

2015

Stephen becomes a Top 10 Finalist for the Global Teacher Prize.

2017

Stephen wins a World Maker Faire Award. It celebrates his work with the Green Bronx Machine.

Depth of Knowledge

1 What are three skills Stephen needed to become a successful teacher?

2 Why is it important to use sustainable methods of gardening?

3 What are some ways Stephen helped his students learn to help others? List two examples using information provided in the book.

4 How can gardening innovations like Tower Gardens help a neighborhood or community?

5 At first, Stephen Ritz did not expect to become a teacher. He received his teaching license after he had to quit playing basketball. What surprises in your life have led to unexpected and exciting new experiences?

6 Write an opinion piece on why people join clubs like the Green Teens. Be sure to include an introduction and a conclusion. Support your point of view with facts from the story.

7 What would you say if your friend asked you how they can lose weight like Stephen did? Write a three-paragraph answer explaining the steps they can take. Include the skills they will need. Use examples from this book.

Grow In Your Classroom

Stephen Ritz taught his class about teamwork when he grew Tower Gardens with his students. Tower Gardens are a big commitment, but you can help your class in a similar way by growing plants together!

STEPS TO TAKE

1 Ask your teacher for permission to grow a set of plants in your classroom.

2 With your teacher's help, decide how many plants your class will grow.

3 Follow the instructions in the Make It Happen! on page 13 to grow your plants.

4 Set up a schedule for watering and taking care of each plant. What needs to be done for each plant on each day of the week?

5 Ask your class for volunteers. Assign each volunteer a specific plant, or a day of the week when it will be their turn to take care of the plants.

After three to four weeks, review how things are going. Are your plants growing? Review the schedule again with your volunteers. Does it need any adjustments? What did growing plants in your classroom teach you about teamwork?

Glossary

academics *(noun)* the classes taken at school or in college (pg. 9)

advisor *(noun)* a person who gives opinions or suggestions to someone about what to do (pg. 21)

career *(noun)* a job or profession that someone does for a long time (pg. 4)

community center *(noun)* a place where people can gather for activities (pg. 8)

creatively *(adverb)* using imagination to think of new ideas (pg. 20)

diverse *(adjective)* made up of many different types of people (pg. 8)

epic *(adjective)* very important, wonderful, or exciting; going beyond what is normal or ordinary (pg. 24)

exceed *(verb)* to go beyond or be greater than something (pg. 15)

generate *(verb)* to produce or create something, such as energy (pg. 24)

hydroponic *(adjective)* relating to a method of gardening where plants are grown in water rather than soil (pg. 21)

initiative *(noun)* the determination to learn new things on your own; the ability to get things done (pg. 13)

innovative *(adjective)* using a new idea or method in order to do something (pg. 23)

innovator *(noun)* someone who uses a new idea or method of doing something (pg. 9)

inspire *(verb)* to give another person the idea or confidence to try something new (pg. 11)

invention *(noun)* a new tool or device that someone came up with to serve a purpose (pg. 12)

license *(noun)* an official document that gives a person permission to do something (pg. 19)

motivate *(verb)* to inspire someone to work hard and be successful (pg. 20)

nurture *(verb)* to take care of or help something or someone grow or succeed (pg. 16)

opportunity *(noun)* a chance to do something you wouldn't otherwise get to do (pg. 15)

poverty *(noun)* the state of being very poor (pg. 16)

skill *(noun)* the ability to do something that comes from training, experience, or practice (pg. 4)

specialist *(noun)* someone who has skill or knowledge about a specific thing; an expert (pg. 20)

sustainable *(adjective)* able to not use up the Earth's natural resources (pg. 23)

teamwork *(noun)* the working together of a group of people in order to achieve something (pg. 8)

technology *(noun)* machines or other tools that were developed using scientific knowledge in order to solve problems (pg. 20)

urban farming *(noun)* growing food in a city or town (pg. 21)

Read More

Chong, Susan Burns. *Community Gardens: Grow Your Own Vegetables and Herbs.* Urban Gardening and Farming for Teens. New York: Rosen Publishing, 2014.

Gold, Rozanne. *Eat Fresh Food: Awesome Recipes for Teen Chefs.* New York: Bloomsbury Children's Books, 2009.

Fry, Stella. *Grandpa's Garden.* Cambridge, MA: Barefoot Books, 2012.

Kamkwamba, William. *The Boy Who Harnessed the Wind: Creating Currents of Electricity and Hope.* New York: William Morrow, 2009.

Lewis, Barbara A. *The Teen Guide to Global Action: How to Connect with Others (Near & Far) to Create Social Change.* Minneapolis: Free Spirit Pub., 2008.

Ritz, Stephen. *The Power of a Plant: A Teacher's Odyssey to Grow Healthy Minds and Schools.* Emmaus, Penn.: Rodale, 2017.

Smith, Remmi. *The Healthy Teen Cookbook: Around the World In 80 Fantastic Recipes.* Coral Gables, FL: Mango Pub. Group, 2017.

Internet Links

https://stephenritz.com/

https://greenbronxmachine.org/

https://twitter.com/stephenritz

https://twitter.com/greenBXmachine

https://www.facebook.com/StephenRitzOfficial/

https://www.facebook.com/green.BX.machine/

https://www.towergarden.com/

https://youtu.be/SGnW16shU8k

https://www.ted.com/talks/stephen_ritz_a_teacher_growing_green_in_the_south_bronx

Bibliography

Adely, Hannan. "Teacher's Dedication Keeps Kids Inspired." Norwood News, The Bronx Mall, 2 Nov. 2000, web. http://www.bronxmall.com/norwoodnews/past/110200/features/page1.html. Accessed 9 Aug. 2018.

Loewe, Emma. "How This Elementary School in the Bronx Is Using Farming as a Vehicle for Change." mindbodygreen, 13 Nov. 2017, web. https://www.mindbodygreen.com/articles/how-this-elementary-school-in-the-bronx-is-using-farming-as-a-vehicle-for-change. Accessed 9 Aug. 2018.

Spaen, Brian. "Teacher From The Bronx Builds A Green Classroom To Improve School Performance." Green Matters, 14 Sep. 2017, web. https://www.greenmatters.com/community/2017/09/14/262LVg/stephen-ritz-green-classroom. Accessed 9 Aug. 2018.

Steussy, Lauren. "How a bunch of daffodils broke up a school fight." New York Post, NYP Holdings, Inc., 2 May 2017, web. https://nypost.com/2017/05/02/how-a-bunch-of-daffodils-broke-up-a-school-fight/. Accessed 9 Aug. 2018.

Wah, Louisa. "The Power of a Plant: Interview with 'People Farmer' Stephen Ritz." *Change Food,* 29 Apr. 2017, web. http://www.changefood.org/2017/04/29/the-power-of-a-plant-interview-with-people-farmer-stephen-ritz/. Accessed 9 Aug. 2018.

Index